£299

PICTURES · FROM · THE · PAST

Cricket

PICTURES · FROM · THE · PAST

Cricket

Nick Yapp

SELECT
EDITIONS

First published in Great Britain in 1991
by Collins & Brown Limited

Text Copyright © Nick Yapp 1991

ISBN 1 85648 129 8

The pictures in this book are archive photographs and, to preserve the character and quality of the original, have not been re-touched in any way.

Acknowledgements
The author and publishers are grateful to the following for permission to reproduce copyright photographs:
S & G Press Agency Ltd: 76–7 (bottom), 89 (top).
George Beldam: 10–11.

All other photographs were supplied by the Hulton Picture Company and are available as framed prints. For more information and to place your orders contact:

Framed Prints
Hulton Picture Company
Unique House
21–31 Woodfield Road
London W9 2BA

Tel: 071 266 2660
Fax: 071 266 2414

This edition published 1993 by
The Promotional Reprint Co Ltd,
exclusively for Selecta Book Ltd,
Folly Road,Roundway, Devizes,
Wiltshire, SN10 2HR

Printed in China

CONTENTS

INTRODUCTION

There were those born in late Victorian England who saw Grace in his prime, Hobbs in *their* prime, the phenomenon of Bradman as they reached the foothills of middle age, and still lived long enough to see England regain the Ashes in 1953.

Until the advent of sponsorship, one day games and knockout competitions in the 1960s, cricket changed little in a lifetime. It grew. Internationally it ceased to be purely an England v Australia concern. The first Test against South Africa was played at Port Elizabeth in March 1889. C. Aubrey Smith ('Round-the-Corner Smith') captained England in his only Test and took 5 for 19 in South Africa's first innings. Nearly twenty years later the West Indies joined the international circuit, to be followed eighteen months later by New Zealand, and, in 1932, by All India – partition of the subcontinent did not take place until August 15 1947, a day on which Compton thrashed the Kent bowling for 168 at Lords.

Cricket was tinkered with: administrators changed regulations concerning the size of stumps, the laws relating to leg before wicket, declarations, fair and unfair bowling, the num-

LEFT: *The Tools of the Trade 1. The best cricket equipment has always been hand-made. Here, Mr H. Pound, forty-five years a ball-maker, was making spare time ammunition for the BEF in February 1940.*

RIGHT: *The Tools of the Trade 2. 'Within the sound of Lords,' ran the caption, 'willow wedges are being used for bats.' The craftsman was Mr Fred Church of Catford, and he had worked here for over half a century.*

ber of points for a win, draw or tie. Bats became heavier, pads and gloves thicker, boots lighter, flannels better fitting. Cricket became more athletic, more technical, more scientific, but it was a steady process, at the speed of an ocean voyage rather than that of a jet flight.

From 1889 to 1953 cricket was *the* sport, the national game – it has 'the majesty of national recreation', according to Charles Alcock, one of its greatest administrators. In the late nineteenth century, crowds flocked in their tens of thousands to Lords and Old Trafford, the Oval and Trent Bridge, Headingley and Edgbaston. The seasons rolled by. Victoria died. Cricket became even more popular in the years leading to the Great War. There was the experiment of Triangular Tests in 1912, and then, from 1914 to 1919, an end to the first class game.

On its return, it was on the basis of two day games that lasted until well into the evening. The move was not popular, particularly with the players themselves, and three day cricket was restored. Through the 1920s and 1930s, the crowds maintained their support, and, in a final flourish of mass attendances, they queued uncomplainingly in the late 1940s.

Then, in the mid 1950s, the crowds began to disappear. They still came for the great occasions, but not for the bread and butter games of the county circuit.

Who did the clerks and porters, shopboys and policemen, soldiers and parsons, actors and MPs flock to see? While the white-haired Gladstone wrestled for the last time with the problem of Home Rule for Ireland, they saw Grace, Fry, Ranji, Tom Hayward, Bobby Abel, Lohmann, Trott, F.S. Jackson and a hundred others. A generation later, recovering from the shock of the first Labour Government, they saw Hobbs and Sutcliffe, Percy Chapman, Woolley, 'Farmer' White, Tate, 'Tich' Freeman, Hammond, Leyland, Hendren and Larwood. Finally, while Australia sent us food parcels and perhaps the best team ever in 1948, they saw such greats as Hutton and Washbrook, Edrich and Compton, Bedser, Evans, Laker, Wardle and Joe Hardstaff junior.

Mirabile dictu, it was an age when England was expected to win, or not to lose, against all but Australia. From Grace to Hutton, England lost only four home Tests, outside the Ashes; one against South Africa in 1935, and three against the wonderful West Indian side of 1950.

There were hiccups. In the winter of 1932–1933, the Bodyline Tour threatened the stability of the Empire:

'Bodyline bowling assumed such proportions as to menace best interests of Game. In our opinion is unsportsmanlike. Unless stopped at once likely to upset friendly relations existing

LEFT: *Wally Hammond. 'It was easy to look into his future; there is no mistaking the thoroughbred. We needn't look for hours at quality … mediocrity needs the proof of print and percentages before it is recognized even as mediocrity. Hammond was born to distinction on the cricket field.' (Sir Neville Cardus)*

between Australia and England.' (Cablegram sent by Australian Board of Control 18.1.1933).

It is said that Larwood's Test career was ended by the intervention of J.H. Thomas, Dominions Secretary in Ramsay Macdonald's National Government. Not until the D'Oliveira affair of 1968 did a cabinet minister again act *in loco selectoris*.

And, finally, there were the great cricket writers. Every national paper had its handful of cricket correspondents and reports were detailed and lengthy. In Australia there were Ray Robinson, Arthur Mailey and Jack Fingleton; in the West Indies the most famous was C.L.R. James; in England there were R.C. Robertson-Glasgow, E.H.D. Sewell, Percy Fender, and R.B. Vincent of *The Times*. But the *doyen* of them all was Neville Cardus, 'Cricketer' of *The Manchester Guardian:* 'I watched Spooner rippling the sunlit grass with strokes that were without solidity or earthly momentum, and he leaned gracefully forward and flicked his wrists and the whole of the June day and the setting of sky and white tents and the trees of Canterbury were as though the created element of this lovely player's every motion and breath of being.'

It seems, sadly, that there is no longer time nor space for such elegant appreciation.

RIGHT: *Fred Trueman. 'He was born with a rhythm for bowling.' (John Woodcock) 'His action was faultless in its body-swing, his bared, sparsely-haired chest affronting the sensibilities of mid-on and his metalled right toe braking the pent-up power of his troublesome final seven-league stride until the last volcanic moment.' (Frank Tyson)*

THE GOLDEN AGE

It was an age of giants. Some were physically enormous: Warwick Armstrong weighed in at twenty-two stone, more than a match for even Grace or Murdoch. Some were tiny: Bobby Abel was known as 'The Mighty Atom'. Big or small they strode to the wicket over rougher turf than we see today, bats dark as ebony, pads thin and hard, gloves so threadbare that wicket keepers slapped a beefsteak inside their gloves for added protection.

The sun always shone. The crowds flocked to see Ranji and Rhodes, Hearne and Hirst, Briggs and Blythe, Lockwood and Lohmann. The calendar was full of cricket: county games, the universities, Gents and Players, North and South, Smokers v Non-Smokers, London County v MCC and Ground, Gentlemen of Philadelphia v Gentlemen of England. Runs were plundered and squandered. Bowlers either had 'hearts too big for their bodies' or were 'demons'.

And, at the centre of it all was W.G. Grace – the Doctor, the 'Grand Old Man', the superhero. A century ago he and Victoria herself were the only two inhabitants of the British Isles instantly recognizable by the rest of the population. In the forty-three years of his career, cricket came of age: the County Championship was constituted, the first Test match was played, cricket statisticians began their obsessive cataloguing. With Grace, modern cricket was born in the orchards of Gloucestershire.

RIGHT: *Ho Statesmen, Patriots, bards make way*
Your fame has sunk to zero:
For Victor Trumper is today
Our one Australian hero.

Creeve Roe

'So much have I read of him, that I am
prepared to believe that nobody, before or
since, ever achieved the standards of
batsmanship set by Trumper.'

(Jack Fingleton)

BELOW: *W.G. Grace and fellow stalwarts of the Golden Age. This isn't an England team, but probably an XI representing the South. The umpire on the right is Bob Thoms, who 'belonged essentially to the sixties, looking exactly like the photographs of some of the players of those days.' (Wisden)*

BELOW: *Frederick Robert Spofforth, the Demon Bowler. 'He had the evil eye; he was tall and angular and satanic of aspect...' (Cardus), but not off the field.*

BELOW: *Warwick Windridge Armstrong coming out to bat against England in 1909. The Hon. Lionel Tennyson considered that Armstrong 'suggested a mountain of geniality.'*

RIGHT: *Charles Burgess Fry, of Sussex, Surrey, Hampshire and England. 'Fry played by the book of arithmetic. He was the acutest thinker ever known to the game; his every stroke was an idea, a principle, and his every innings a synthesis.' (Cardus)*

BELOW: *Albert Craig, the Surrey Laureate, peddling his poetry at the Oval. Craig improvised rhymes about games in progress, and sold broadsheets of cricketing verses of a sub-McGonigall quality:*
Darling Old Oval, once again we meet,
One clan to triumph, one to bear defeat...

LEFT: *Kumar Shri Ranjitsinhji. 'One would not be surprised to see a brown curve burnt in the grass where one of his cuts has travelled, or see blue flame shiver around his bat in the making of one of those leg-strokes.' (C.B. Fry)*

RIGHT: *Tom Richardson. 'Richardson had a physique of iron, an unconquerable spirit, which bowled itself to a standstill by 6.30 and came back next morning ready to try again.' (C.L.R. James)*

BELOW: *William Henry Lockwood (left) and Robert Peel. They played together in only one home Test. MacLaren regarded Peel as the greatest left hander of his time. Fry reckoned Lockwood on his best form a tougher proposition than Richardson.*

BELOW RIGHT: *Archibald Campbell MacLaren. 'Archie goes in to bat armed at all points, able and ready to meet any bowling upon any wicket. No one was ever less a fairweather batsman.' (C.B. Fry) On July 16, 1895, while the sun shone, MacLaren made 424 against Somerset at Taunton.*

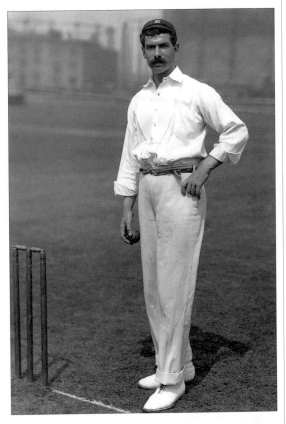

ABOVE: *27.5.1909. England v Australia at Edgbaston. MacLaren and Tyldesley are batting: MacLaren will not last much longer.*

RIGHT: *31.3.1914. Return of the MCC from South Africa. On the quayside are Mr and Mrs J.W. Hearne (left) and Mr and Mrs E.J. Smith. They were probably pleased to be home: neither had had a wonderful tour.*

RIGHT: *Sydney Francis Barnes. He was plucked from the Lancashire League to play his first game for England, and his first wicket was Trumper, caught and bowled for 2 at Sydney. To many Barnes remains the greatest bowler ever.*

ABOVE: *July 1914. The Grand Old Man at Eltham Cricket Club in the last few days of the Golden Age. A few weeks later Grace wrote to* The Sportsman: *'The fighting on the Continent is very severe . . . I think the time has arrived when the county cricket season should be closed, for it is not fitting at a time like this that able-bodied men should be playing day after day and pleasure seekers look on. . . .'*

BELOW: *Colin Blythe. There is a monument to him on the ground at Canterbury: 'He was unsurpassed among the famous bowlers of his day and beloved by his fellow cricketers.' Blythe was killed at Passchendaele in 1917.*

THE MASTERS

The Master was Jack Hobbs. No one will ever score as many runs or hit as many centuries, but he earned his title not for what he did, but how he played. 'Summer time means Oval time and Oval time means Hobbs' ran the parody, and with Hobbs went Sutcliffe or Sandham or Wilfred Rhodes, who turned out for England in the blistering heat of Sabina Park in a timeless Test at the age of 52 years and 165 days, to bowl 45 overs for 39 runs while the rest of the England attack was cut to pieces.

Hobbs and Sutcliffe were the most famous of many masterly pairs, but there were also Larwood and Voce, Ponsford and Woodfull, Constantine and Francis, Bradman and McCabe, McDonald and Gregory. In December 1928 England fielded a team that many consider their greatest ever. In batting order it was: Hobbs, Sutcliffe, Hammond, Chapman, Hendren, Jardine, Geary, Tate, Larwood, Duckworth and White. They won.

Each of the masters had his own trademark, his *coup* (or hook or drive) *de grace*. And at least one master had every shot in the book. 'In describing a great innings by Woolley,' wrote R.C. Robertson-Glasgow, 'you had to go careful with your adjectives and stack them in little rows, like pats of butter or razor blades. In the first over ... there had been an exquisite off-drive, followed by a perfect cut, then an effortless leg-glance. In the second over the same sort of thing happened; and your superlatives had already gone.'

RIGHT: *12.7.1926. Hobbs and Sutcliffe opening for England against Australia at Headingley. They put on 59 together in the first innings and 156 in the second, when England achieved a comfortable draw.*

BELOW: *Jack Hobbs – 'The Master'. 'He was seldom seen to perform a hurried stroke. I never saw him guilty of an ugly, ungrammatical stroke. He would lose his wicket, being human, by error of judgment, producing the right stroke for the wrong ball.' (Cardus)*

FAR RIGHT: *Andrew Sandham. He made 107 hundreds, and 63 century partnerships with Jack Hobbs. Few batsmen of his achievements have received less notice.*

RIGHT: *3.5.1939. Frank Woolley batting for Les Ames's XI against the West Indians at Gravesend, towards the end of his career. He made 59 before being bowled by Stollmeyer. It was a typical Woolley innings.*

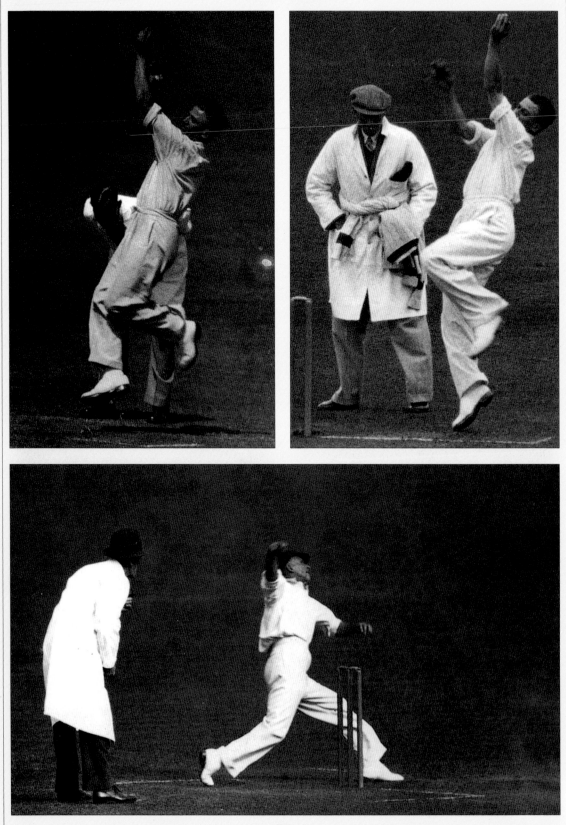

Bowlers

It was not an age for bowlers. The wickets were hard and unyielding. In England, there were twenty triple centuries in as many years. In Australia, Victoria twice totalled more than a thousand runs. The great fast bowlers came in pairs, but the great slow bowlers plied their craft as individuals: Mailey, Fender, Verity, Freeman and Wilfred Rhodes.

LEFT AND FAR LEFT: *August 1936. Larwood bowling against Surrey at the Oval. Like all the great bowlers, Larwood relied on imperceptible changes of his action to deceive batsmen. 'He was the last of the classical fast bowlers.' (Cardus)*

RIGHT: *William Joseph O'Reilly bowling at the Oval in 1938, 'territorially distinct in rhythm, passion, scheme and transition.' (Edmund Blunden)*

LEFT: *Clarence Victor Grimmett. 'Grimmett with a straight, quick, skippety run of half a dozen paces. He bowled with his shoulders hunched. His arm whipped round like a boxer's right swing. He is the nearest to a round-arm bowler seen in big cricket since they ceased pressing trousers out sideways.'*
(Ray Robinson)

LEFT: *15.7.1930. Maurice Tate and Percy Chapman walk out to face Australia at Headingley. They put on 51 together but were unable to save the follow-on. Few cricketers today manage to look so happy in such circumstances.*

LEFT: *Charles George Macartney at Old Trafford in 1926. He scored 109 that day. In the previous Test at Lords, he had made 112 before lunch on the first day.*

RIGHT: *Lupton, Hirst and Rhodes. The deeds of Rhodes and Hirst are well enough known, but Arthur William Lupton is less famous. He was a hard-hitting lower order left-hand bat and a right-arm fast-medium bowler who captained Yorkshire from 1925 to 1927.*

LEFT: *Patsy Hendren coming out to bat through a crowd of admirers. 'Hendren has deserved his place in every Test match or MCC tour for which he has been selected, though had he been a lesser player his unfailing good spirits, his jolly wit, and an ability to play the clown without hurting anyone's feelings would have told greatly in his favour as a good companion.' (The Times 23.5.31)*

RIGHT: *Learie Nicholas Constantine. 'He hit with great power and certainty, bowled at an intimidating pace, and was dazzling in the slips.' (C.L.R. James)*

LEFT: *25.7.1939. George Headley – The Black Bradman – batting against England at Old Trafford. He was graceful and aggressive: 'What is this business of opening batsmen batting for two hours and making 40 or 60 runs?'*

BELOW: *Kenneth Farnes (left) and Hedley Verity (right) are greeted by Farnes's father at Waterloo Station on their return from touring South Africa in March 1939. They each had one more summer of cricket before the war ended their careers and their lives.*

THE COUNTY CIRCUIT

Wisden shows that county cricket between the Wars was dominated by Yorkshire and Lancashire, but the camera preserves what the records cannot in the drama, humour and intensity of the bread and butter cricket of the professional – when he was allowed to play. In 1919 many counties still fielded largely amateur sides. When Somerset tied with Sussex in May of that year (Mr H.J. Heygate's rheumatism being such that he was dismissed for taking over two minutes to reach the wicket), fourteen of the twenty-two players were 'Gentlemen'.

In England alone some six or seven thousand first class games were played between 1919 and 1939. Some were the set piece Bank Holiday matches: Yorkshire and Lancashire, Surrey and Notts, Middlesex and Sussex. Some ended in a day, some in a tie, some in a staggering change of fortune: Hampshire beat Warwickshire by 155 runs at Edgbaston in June 1922, after being dismissed in their first innings for 15.

But the vast majority of those games are forgotten, and the players with them. How many remember Sibbles of Lancashire, Clugston of Warwickshire, Beet of Derbyshire or Fairservice of Kent? Some had at least one day in the headlines: Keeton, Ashdown and Ducat all hit triple centuries; Collins, Smailes, Watts and Mercer took all ten wickets in an innings. Hallows played only twice for England, but on the circuit in 1928, he scored a thousand runs before the end of May.

RIGHT: *The Kent county side in 1925. Back row, left to right: Wright, Hardinge, Woolley. Middle row: Day, Cornwallis, Deed, Hubble. Front row: Ashdown, Seymour, Freeman, Collins.*

Champion County

It was a different championship, where a
county played every other county twice in a
season. Wickets were uncovered. Travel was
largely by steam train. And only a handful of
counties could hope to win: Lancashire,
Surrey, Middlesex, Notts or Derbyshire. Above
all, there was Yorkshire, who won the
championship in 1919, four years running in
the 1920s and seven years out of ten during the
1930s.

RIGHT: *15.6.1932. Holmes and Sutcliffe walking
out to open for Yorkshire against Essex at
Leyton. By the end of the day they had put on
over 400 together.*

FAR RIGHT: *Maurice Leyland batting in 1935.
'Leyland persisted, and conquered by his rare
character.' (Cardus) He was the backbone of
the Yorkshire batting during many of their
championship years.*

LEFT: *16.6.1932. The
Leyton scoreboard at
the end of the
partnership between
Holmes and Sutcliffe.
They were together at
the crease for 445
minutes. Essex were
then dismissed for 78
and 164, Verity taking
5 for 8 and 5 for 45.*

In 1935 Yorkshire were unbeaten until August. It was a team that could have represented England: Hutton, Sutcliffe, Barber, Leyland, Sellars, Verity, Bowes, Wood, Mitchell, Smailes and Turner. Throughout Yorkshire's championship years, there were those at Bramhall Lane, Bradford and Headingley who felt there was scarce room for Jack Hobbs in the national side.

ABOVE: *15.9.1935. Yorkshire Celebration Dinner at the Savoy Hotel, London. Sir Charles Sykes is making the presentation to A.B. Sellers, Yorkshire's captain. Also to be seen are Sutcliffe, Bowes, Verity, Barber and Leyland.*

RIGHT: *17.9.1935. Verity bowling for The Champion County v The Rest at the Oval. It was the first time in thirty years that a Champion County won this fixture, and Verity played a big part in Yorkshire's victory.*

LEFT: *6.8.1925. Ladies Day at the Canterbury Festival. Left to right: Mr R.H. Marriott, Mr C.W.M. Kemp, A.E.R. Gilligan and Mrs R.H. Marriott.*

RIGHT: *Charles Stowell Marriott in 1927. 'Father' Marriott played in only one Test, against the West Indies at the Oval in 1933 where he took 11 for 96. As a teacher at Dulwich, his first class cricket was usually limited to the summer holidays.*

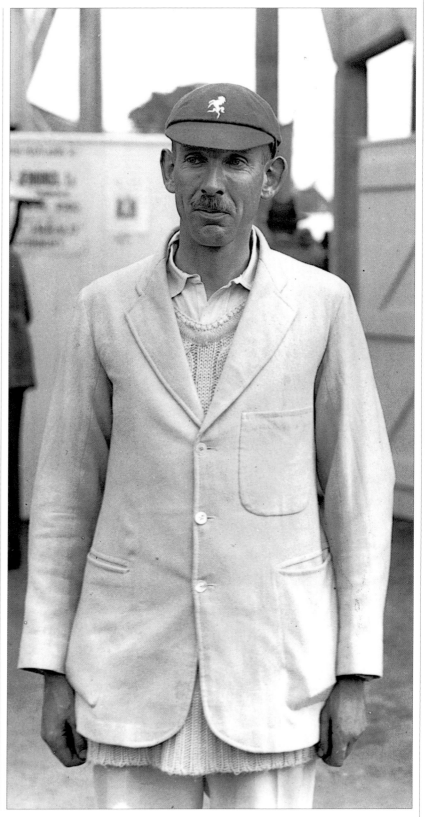

LEFT: *17.8.1925. Jack Hobbs raises his glass to the Taunton crowd after scoring his 126th hundred and equalling Grace's record. 'He raised his glass high and bowed to the crowd.' (Wisden) The following day he scored a second hundred.*

Fielding

If there has ever been a golden age of fielding, it is in the present rather than the past. 'Men stand in the field today like so many waxen figures in a tailor's shop . . . Today the ball is driven through the so-called fieldsmen . . . and (they) stand facing each other with a lingering hope in their eyes that they will not be compelled to fetch it . . .' Digby Loder Armroid Jephson – *Fielding in the Golden Age*.

Mid-on traditionally used boot rather than hand, but there were honourable exceptions: Hobbs, Bradman, Constantine and Hammond. 'Wally!' said Patsy Hendren, 'He pulled 'em out of the air as if with a hummingbird's tongue.'

RIGHT: *2.8.1952. Clay of Notts is caught by Surridge off Bedser in the traditional Bank Holiday fixture.*

BELOW: *4.7.1953. An airborne Trueman, grounding neither bat nor feet, is run out by Fletcher.*

BOTTOM: *Fender and Garland Wells between them drop Stan McCabe*

ABOVE: *15.7.1933. Kent v Surrey at Blackheath, a local derby which always attracted a large crowd. Despite Hobbs scoring his 194th century, Kent won this game comfortably. Blackheath was not a happy hunting ground for Surrey.*

RIGHT: *The County Ground at Hove – Sussex v Yorkshire, August 1938. Between the wars, Sussex were famous for the relatives in the team: cousins, brothers, fathers and sons.*

ABOVE: *R.A. Sinfield batting for Gloucestershire against Essex at Leyton in August 1927. Then, as now, Essex were a peripatetic side, playing home games at Chelmsford, Leyton, Southend, Brentwood and Colchester. Perhaps that accounts for the sparse attendance.*

THE BRADMAN ERA 1930–1945

'Bradman has to be accepted as we accept the Atlantic Ocean or the five shilling income tax. It cannot be helped.' – C.L.R. James, *Glasgow Herald* April 28, 1937.

He had little over a dozen years of first class cricket, scored 117 centuries, smashed over 300 runs in a single day against England, and came within a square cut of averaging 100 in Tests. He was as famous as Grace, as instantly recognizable on the street as he was on a cricket ground, and people flocked to him as quickly off the field as they spread out when he came to the wicket.

He had an amazing eye, he saw the ball very early, and the eye flashed to the brain what steps should be taken. In turn, those steps were swiftly executed. 'He was blessed with small and beautifully neat feet, which a Pavlova might have envied, and which made him quite exceptionally quick in moving back or forward to the ball.' (P.F. Warner)

He was a phenomenon. The most efficient run machine in the history of the game, as near to faultless in technique as it is possible to be. And yet . . . he never touched the hearts of those who wrote about him. There is warmth and glowing admiration in the way Cardus, Robinson, Sewell, Ross, Swanton and Arlott wrote about Trumper, Hobbs, Mailey, O'Reilly, Hendren and a hundred others. For 'The Don' there was only awe. Maybe he was too good. For most of his career, 'Bradman 0' made for more news than 'Bradman 100.'

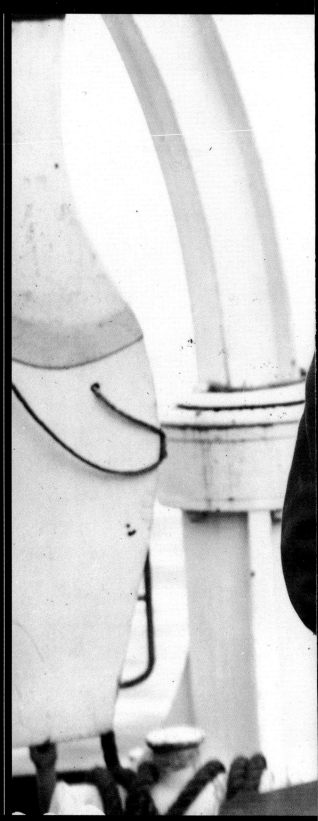

RIGHT: *23.4.1930. The young Bradman arrives by cross channel ferry at Dover for his first tour of England. A week later he smashed a double century at Worcester in the opening match of the tour.*

LEFT: *19.8.1930. England v Australia at the Oval. 'Bradman's innings became more and more impressive as it went on. It was as quiet as his innings at Leeds was energetic . . . We have now seen Bradman the brilliant and Bradman the shrewd.' (Cardus)*

RIGHT: *11.6.1948. England v Australia at Trent Bridge, Bradman's 28th Test century. His pull shot was vicious. And yet . . . 'After the first excitement, this sort of thing becomes slightly monotonous. A bowler bowls, Bradman makes a stroke, not a single fieldsman moves, and the ball is returned from the boundary.' (C.L.R. James)*

LEFT: *12.7.1930. Bradman returns to the pavilion after scoring 334 against England at Headingley. He had scored 309 runs the previous day – still a world record.*

The Bodyline Tour

'The firing of the first cannon-ball in the history of warfare did not cause as much consternation as Larwood's first fast ball bowled past the batsman's left ear to a crouching leg trap.' (Cardus)

It nearly came to blows, Australia threatened to leave the Commonwealth, and careers were ruined. It began before the tour itself, but reached its Antipodean apogee at Adelaide on January 14 1933. That day, Woodfull was struck over the heart, Oldfield's skull was fractured, and Bradman was dismissed for 8.

TOP: *26.9.1932. Before the storm: Voce, Mitchell and Larwood limbering up on board the Orient liner* Orontes *en route to Australia.*

TOP RIGHT: *27.1.1933. Jardine leads out the England team for the second Test at Melbourne. The fireworks were yet to come.*

RIGHT: *15.3.1933. Woodfull ducks a ball from Larwood during the fourth Test at Brisbane. By this time, relations between the two countries were decidedly strained.*

'The first dorsal interosseous muscle, between the thumb and index finger, ached for a week after batting against Larwood, so severe was the concussion of the ball hitting the bat. I experienced this against no other fast bowler.' (Jack Fingleton)

Larwood was fast and accurate, the bullet fired from Jardine's gun. England won the series by four matches to one. On their return, they were congratulated, fêted, rewarded.

RIGHT: *13.2.1933. Eddie Paynter hits out at Brisbane in the fourth Test. He had left his hospital bed with a temperature of 102 'to save his side from the imminent threat of defeat.' (The Times) He made 83 in four hours and England regained the Ashes.*

RIGHT: *30.12.1932. Bradman's first duck in Test cricket. In attempting to hook Bowes, Bradman leapt across his wicket but dragged the ball on to his stumps. In the second innings he scored 103 not out.*

RIGHT: *All over bar the incriminations. Jardine presents certificates to Larwood and Voce back home at Trent Bridge. 'Jardine's book did not help matters,' wrote Plum Warner. 'Larwood might well have said "Save me from my friends" – and he had some pretty bad ones!'*

LEFT: *The post war Bradman. His cutting was still ruthless though maybe some of the hunger for runs had gone. Evans and Edrich wait in vain.*

BELOW: *30.4.1938. Yet another Bradman century at Worcester. A telegraph boy brings a telegram of congratulations to the wicket.*

ABOVE: *23.6.1938. Bradman off duty at Wimbledon on the day before the Lords Test.*

The Oval, August 1938

It was to be a timeless Test. The last time England and Australia had met at the Oval, in 1934, Australia had won by 562 runs. The revenge was grotesque rather than sweet.

It was nightmarish. When the England score was somewhere between 700 and 800, Cardus wrote: 'A new game has been invented which employs the implements of cricket.' Woodfull is said to have asked about the effects of snow on the wicket. Some Chelsea pensioners watching wondered how many of them would live to see the end of the match.

RIGHT: *20.8.1938. Bradman and Hammond spinning a coin. Bradman lost and England batted first. Between the two captains is Bosser Martin, the Oval groundsman.*

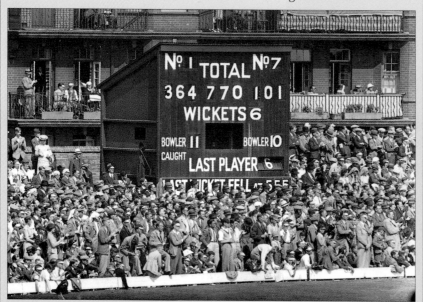

ABOVE: *23.8.1938. The Oval scoreboard early on the third day. Hutton has just been dismissed, and the crowd are still standing in recognition and, perhaps, relief.*

LEFT: *23.8.1938. Hutton receives congratulations from Bradman and others after passing Bradman's previous record score.*

It was all over in four days. Bradman made a rare tactical error and selected only three bowlers for the Australian team. Between them they bowled 242 overs and took 5 for 626. For Fleetwood-Smith (1 for 298) it was the end. 'On a fair pitch,' wrote Cardus, 'he would have taken wickets; his fine art was abused by the groundsman's drowsy syrups.'

Bradman himself bowled fourteen balls, and then wrenched his ankle. He took no further part in the match.

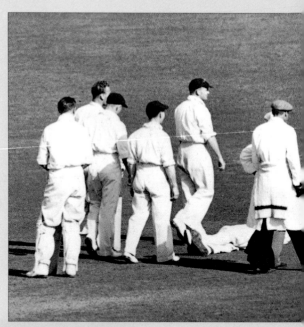

RIGHT: *23.8.1938. Bradman is carried from the field and Australia drain the dregs of cricketing misery.*

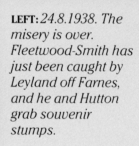

LEFT: *24.8.1938. The misery is over. Fleetwood-Smith has just been caught by Leyland off Farnes, and he and Hutton grab souvenir stumps.*

TOP RIGHT: *24.8.1938. The crowd covers the ground. 'On the fourth day, the proceedings were so one-sided as to be almost farcical,'* (Wisden) *but the takings were a record for the Oval.*

RIGHT: *24.8.1938. The victorious England team. Back row, left to right: Edrich, Fagg, Bowes, Hutton, Hardstaff, Compton, Wood. Front row: Verity, Farnes, Hammond, Leyland, Paynter.*

RIGHT: *Bradman maintained his masterly technique by practice. Here he is warming up in the nets at Trent Bridge in June 1938. He had a reasonable game – 195 runs for once out.*

LEFT: *14.8.1948. England v Australia at the Oval, Bradman's last Test match innings. Yardley calls for three cheers as 'The Don' arrives at the wicket.*

ABOVE: *14.8.1938. Two balls later: Bradman's last duck in Test cricket, bowled by a googly from Hollies. Bradman claimed he was not overcome by the emotion of the occasion, but Evans, who was nearest to him at the time, has said otherwise.*

Gentlemen and Players

The origins of cricket were as much rustic and ecclesiastical as gentlemanly, but the game was refined by Noblemen and Gentry from White Conduit Fields and the New Road, Mary-le-Bone. Gentlemen and Players, amateurs and professionals – the line between them was clearly drawn. They were distinguished, the one from the other, on scorecards. They changed separately, dined separately, entered the field of play through separate gates.

Cricket was ruled and administered by gentlemen. Not until 1952 did a professional captain England, and even then he was banned from captaining his county. The professional called his skipper 'sir', referred to him as 'Mr ...' and took his orders without argument. Larwood, who learnt his cricket bowling with lumps of stone on industrial wasteland, did as he was told by Mr Jardine, who learnt his cricket on the playing fields of Winchester.

At the top were Lord Hawke and Lord Harris, both a little eccentric. Lord Hawke ruled Yorkshire cricket as a benevolent despot. 'His contribution to the game was great ... but he sometimes dwelt too much in the past ... For one who had travelled so far ... it was curious that he was not always anxious to welcome Australian teams.' (P.F. Warner).

As for Lord Harris, one of his less happy successes was that of preventing the young Hammond playing for Gloucestershire for a whole season on the grounds that: 'Bolshevism is rampant ... and this year cricket has not escaped its attack.'

RIGHT: *1.5.1923. Cricketers from Barbados, Trinidad, Demerara and Jamaica arrive at London's West India Dock. The caption helpfully states: 'Their captain, H.G.B. Austin, is wearing a light coat.' A great many years were to pass before the West Indies were to have a black captain.*

LEFT: *Harry Makepeace steps out with some of his cricketing apprentices at Old Trafford in March 1948. Makepeace was one of Cardus's favourite cricketers; he described him as Lancashire's Danton.*

ABOVE: *11.7.1940. Patsy Hendren coaches two Harrovians in the week before their match against Eton. Though they look vastly superior, they must have taken some of his advice. In the match D.F. Henley (centre) 'struck a brilliant streak of bowling' (Wisden) and finished with 6 for 36. J.F. Godsell (left) took 2 for 49, but Eton won by 1 wicket.*

BELOW: *15.7.1935. Country house cricket at Penshurst Castle. Mrs Ken Homan chatting to some of her friends during the interval.*

RIGHT: *The Gifted Amateur. Kumar Shri Duleepsinhji hitting out against Australia at the Oval in August 1930. Like his uncle, the great Ranji, Duleep played for Sussex and England.*

BELOW RIGHT: *The Solid Professional. George Gunn junior batting for Notts in 1937. Both his father and his uncle played for the same county.*

RIGHT: *Lord Harris greets members of the MCC party on their return from Australia at Dover in April 1929. Warner found his Lordship 'a little* difficile'. *Certainly Harris was a man of strange utterances.*

LEFT: *12.7.1946. Eton comes to London. Supporters arrive for the game against Harrow at Lords. 'Like Ascot, this year's Eton and Harrow game was on austerity lines and missing from the display were the familiar top hats of the Eton schoolboys and the straw boaters of the boys from Harrow School.'*

TOP RIGHT: *18.8.1942. London comes to Eton. Eight hundred youngsters from the Boys' Brigade were allowed to camp and play on Agar's Plough. The caption reads: 'Two of the happy little Londoners coming out to play cricket on the Eton cricket pitch. Left is Eric Innocent, aged 13, and, right, Ron Curtis, both from Ilford.'*

RIGHT: *One of the great events of the social calendar: Oxford v Cambridge at Lords, June 1909. That month* The Times *decried the tea interval at cricket matches, but the Varsity Match was different.*

FIELDS OF PLAY

Many writers on cricket claimed that the game was shaped by its surroundings. The heart of the game was to be found in the partisan crowds at county headquarters – Taunton and Worcester, Chelmsford and Maidstone, Old Trafford and Trent Bridge – grounds where you paid three bob to enter, hired a cushion for sixpence, bought an up-to-date scorecard, and where there was not an advertising hoarding to be seen. At Festival time, in Scarborough, Folkestone or Blackpool, however, batsmen threw caution and suspicion to the sea-scented winds, no longer the careful plodders who had taken three hours over fifty at Leicester or Derby.

Lords was always *the* ground, the sacred city. 'Of that city,' according to a *Times* leading article of September 7, 1929, 'the Pavilion is the temple. Valhalla is perhaps the better word . . . There is a sanctuary undesecrated by the foot of woman, one of the last asylums of the merely male in an epicene world.'

And, away across the oceans were the vast amphitheatres of Australia, where massive crowds, three times the size of that at Lords, 'dwarfed the sense of personal identity'. They reminded Cardus of drawings by Fougasse.

RIGHT: *A general view of what many regard as the essence of English county cricket: the ground at Worcester.*

ABOVE: *1.1.1929. The birthplace of cricket: Broadhalfpenny Down, Hambledon. This New Year's Day game was between the Invalids, captained by J.C. Squire, and the Hampshire Eskimos, captained by E. Whalley-Tooker. The Invalids won by 11 runs, on a day that,* The Times *recorded, gave 'the illusion it had been carefully picked and stolen from history.'*

RIGHT: *The largest cricket ground in the world: the MCG, Melbourne, Australia. Its modest forerunner staged the first Test ever in 1877.*

BELOW: *Old Trafford, July 1924. A lone spectator waits for play in the Test match against South Africa. There won't be any; not another ball was bowled.*

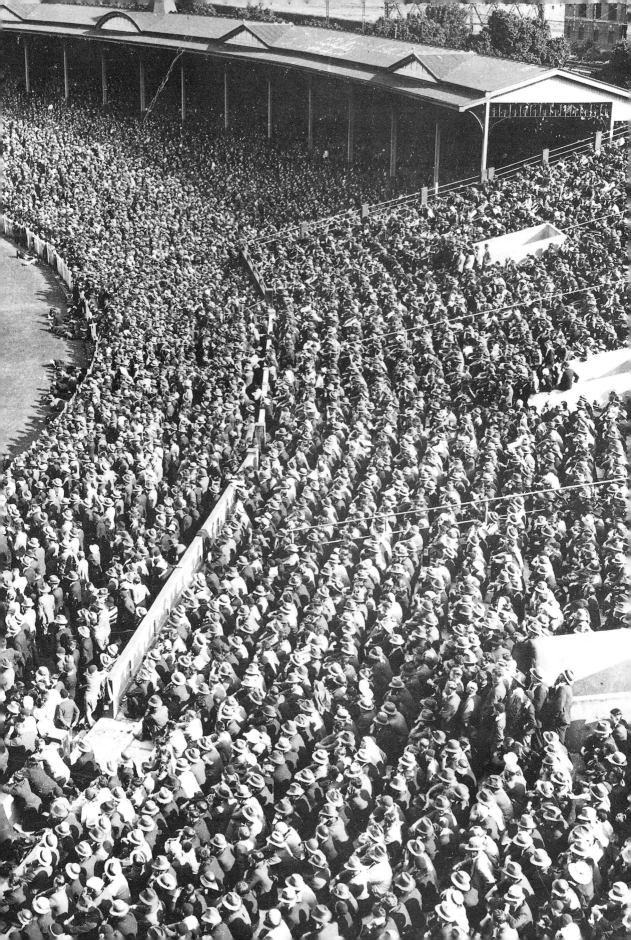

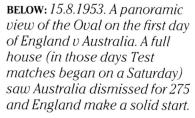

BELOW: *15.8.1953. A panoramic view of the Oval on the first day of England v Australia. A full house (in those days Test matches began on a Saturday) saw Australia dismissed for 275 and England make a solid start.*

ABOVE: *26.8.1933. The Army v the West Indians on the ground of the Officers Club, Aldershot. It was a three day game, and the first time an overseas team had played on the ground.*

ABOVE: *The Roses Match: Lancashire v. Yorkshire at Old Trafford. No quarter given. 'There was a decade, 1929–1939, when the wicket at Old Trafford was so much a batsman's feather-bed, stuffed with runs, that the Lancashire and Yorkshire match seldom was finished; the argument concentrated on a first innings decision.' (Cardus)*

ABOVE: *9.5.1953. A beautiful Carl Sutton photograph of cricket played on a wasteland near Headingley. It was on surroundings like these that Larwood and Trueman learnt their cricket.*

BELOW: *A panoramic view of the headquarters of cricket, Lords.*

YOUNG BLOOD

The old masters lasted only a year or two into the peace of the 1940s. Leyland and Sutcliffe played another season for Yorkshire, Hammond one more for Gloucestershire. There were new heroes, new giants, new masters. The glorious summer of 1947 made Compton and Edrich household names as they broke record after record, taking England and Middlesex to victory. Not since the Doctor had there been so famous a cricketer as Denis Compton.

Australia routed England the following year with perhaps the best team ever. Bradman was still there, and Barnes, Morris, Hassett, Miller, Harvey, Lindwall and Johnston. For many years Alec Victor Bedser *was* the England attack, bowling from the time the dew was scarce lifted from the ground to the time when it began to settle again. Standing up to Bedser, behind the stumps, was Evans: 'the most unquenchable man in all cricket . . . Never surely was a cricketer so boiling over with vitality or so prodigal of energy.' (Arlott)

There was Jim Laker, walking back to his mark, looking up, as though some god of bowling was signalling from the roof of the pavilion, licking his fingers, and turning to take a few rolling steps back to the bowling crease.

And then, as the era neared its end, as Bill Haley and television and the last of food rationing took us into a different world, there appeared a young Yorkshire lad named Trueman. 'He was puissant in back and long in arm, just like all the mining fast bowlers . . . Yorkshire, Derbyshire and Nottinghamshire have whistled up to the surface. He was the Cassius Clay of fast bowling.' (Frank Tyson)

RIGHT: *Alec Bedser's delivery stride. 'You always knew when Alec was in the mood. His head would start to bob about as he came in from his mark. Sometimes the earth would seem to shake. No one was safe on such days as these.' (John Woodcock)*

LEFT: *Compton (left) and Hendren walk out to bat for Middlesex against Surrey, 1936. At that time Hendren was still the Middlesex number four. Two years later, Compton had taken over from him.*

RIGHT: *Wally Hammond padding up in his England blazer, 1946. It was his last Test series in England. He never regained his pre-war form.*

BELOW: *23.5.1946. Surrey v Old England at the Oval. King George VI is shaking hands with Freeman. 15,000 people attended the one day match to celebrate the Centenary of the Surrey Club and of the Oval as a cricket ground.*

Hutton and Washbrook

For sixteen years the selectors juggled with pairs of England opening batsmen once the old firm of Hobbs and Sutcliffe went into liquidation. Then, in June 1946, Hutton and Washbrook opened against India at Lords. They were a well matched couple: both from the north, both tough, both mean in their possession of the crease. In the opinion of many, they served England 'pretty well', and for five years at least the selectors gave up juggling.

RIGHT: *16.8.1947. Hutton in happier mood, hitting out against the South Africans at the Oval. The Times threatened that it was an innings that 'might well have lasted to eternity', as had his innings nine years earlier.*

ABOVE: *10.6.1948. Hutton and Washbrook walking out to open for England against Australia at Trent Bridge. Apart from the game at Headingley, where they made two century opening partnerships, this was their most disappointing series.*

LEFT: *Cyril Washbrook. He was always a pugnacious batsman: 'Washbrook reminded us that in the right hands a bat is a sword, not a shield.' (C.L.R. James)*

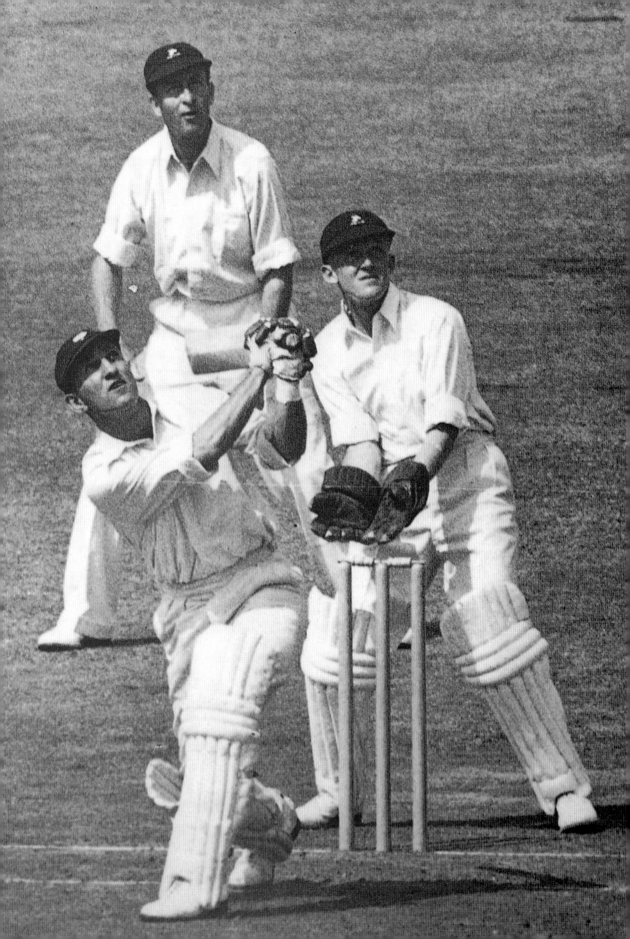

Edrich and Compton

Their *annus mirabilis* was 1947. They broke Hobbs' record for the most centuries in a season and Hayward's record for the most runs in a season. That year, in Tests, Compton averaged 94, Edrich 112. Their one problem was running between the wickets. 'There are too many days when Denis and Bill Edrich seem to find it impossible to run smoothly, and each in turn sends the other back when the run could have been taken in a gentle canter.' (Swanton)

TOP RIGHT: *11.6.1947. Smith is the victim of a beautiful off drive by Compton, who went on to score 163.*

BOTTOM RIGHT: *10.6.1947. England v South Africa at Trent Bridge. Edrich drives Vivian Smith for 4.*

ABOVE: *15.9.1947. Edrich and Compton coming out to bat for Middlesex (Champion County) against The Rest at the Oval. It was the last caning they gave bowlers that summer. Edrich made 180 and Compton, despite knee trouble, 246.*

RIGHT: *15.8.1947. No Government Health warnings in those days. Edrich pads up in the dressing room at Lords on the last day of the match against Kent. It was one of the few that Middlesex lost that year.*

ABOVE: *'Fiery' Fred Trueman. 'He was the Cassius Clay of fast bowling and whilst he did not always state that he was the greatest, one always felt that his mastery was founded on this confidence.' (Frank Tyson)*

RIGHT: *Frank 'Typhoon' Tyson. He watched Ray Lindwall, and learnt the value of speed and length from a shorter run-up.*

ABOVE: *Middlesex had Edrich and Compton: the Surrey twins were Lock and Laker. As he approached the bowling crease, Lock's arm was as clearly jointed as an artist's lay figure.*

RIGHT: *Jim Laker. Metaphorically, Laker wore his spinning finger to the bone for Surrey and England: in reality, it blistered and hardened to twice its normal size.*

The West Indies at Lords, June 1950

With those little pals of mine,
Ramadhin and Valentine . . .

West Indian cricket came of age. It was the first time they had beaten England in England, and the victory was by 326 runs. Ramadhin had played only two first class matches prior to the tour, Valentine scarcely more. Between them on this one Test, they bowled 231 overs and took 18 for 279. West Indian cricket was never the same again.

RIGHT: *29.6.1950. The game was over, but the celebrations went on and on. Calypso singer and supporters at Lords.*

LEFT: *'Valentine comes around the wicket with four long, bent-kneed strides, like Groucho Marx getting into the lift before the door closes... As the ball leaves his hand, his forefinger pokes after it – pointing the bone at the batsman.' (Ray Robinson)*

RIGHT: *Sonny Ramadhin. 'The bewitched ball darts from the pitch, mostly whipping back from the off. Occasionally Ramadhin releases a slower ball which looks as if it will be a full toss but dips late in its flight.' (Ray Robinson)*

The match, indeed the whole tour, also saw what C.L.R. James has described as the 'triple efflorescence' of the three Ws: Worrell, Weekes and Walcott, born within a few miles and a few months of each other on the island of Barbados. James once wrote to Worrell: 'I have nothing to write except that I perpetually wonder that a little scrap of West Indian territory has produced Garfield Sobers and you'

BELOW: *Clyde Walcott. Of the three 'W's, he was the most awesomely powerful, with an amazing agility, first earning his place in the West Indies team as a wicket keeper.*

BELOW: *21.7.1950. Salt in the wound: West Indies win at Trent Bridge by ten wickets. Frank Worrell acknowledges the cheers of the crowd on reaching his double century.*

FAR RIGHT: *Everton de Courcy Weekes. He shared in a stand of 283 with Worrell in the third Test at Trent Bridge. 'There was Everton, thick and square and full of muscle...' (E.W. Swanton)*

End of an Era: The Oval, August 1953

The first four Tests in the series were all drawn, though it had taken an innings of granite imobility and some questionable leg theory bowling by Trevor Bailey to save England at Headingley. Hutton, England's first professional captain, lost the toss in all five Tests; Bedser broke Tate's record by taking 39 wickets in the series; and television covered the nail-biting last session.

FAR RIGHT: *Keith Miller. 'He brings boys' dreams to life. He is the cricketer they would all like to be, the one who can hit more gloriously and bowl faster than anybody on earth.' (Ray Robinson)*

RIGHT: *Ray Lindwall. 'He bowled batsmen out. He had them caught and leg before. But, above everything else, he first thought them out.' (Denys Rowbotham)*

BELOW: *18.8.1953. The writing is on the wall. Lock bowls Harvey for 1 in the Australian second innings.*

It had taken England nineteen years to regain the Ashes Edrich and Compton were in at the kill, the last time they batted together in a Test match. The following day a *Times* Leader enthused: 'No cricket season has seen a series of Test matches played more closely in the spirit of the clubs and villages from north of the Trent to south of Sydney on which the health – and the fun – of the game depends.'

ABOVE: *19.8.1953. Hutton acknowledges the crowd from the Oval balcony. 'Both captains addressed the crowd, stressing the excellent spirit in which all the matches had been contested both on and off the field.'* (Wisden)

LEFT: *19.8.1953. Compton sweeps Morris to the boundary and England win by 8 wickets. 'It is natural, after so long and at times so bleak an interval, for lovers of English cricket to rejoice.'* (The Times *20.8.1953*).

BELOW: *19.8.1953. The victorious England team. Back row, left to right: Bailey, May, Graveney, Laker, Lock, Wardle (twelfth man), Trueman. Front row: Edrich, Bedser, Hutton, Compton, Evans.*

ABOVE: *22.8.1939. The last day of the last Test before the Second World War. Ten days later, German troops crossed the Polish frontier. Martindale (left) and Sealy leave the Oval as the late summer shadows lengthen. It was their final Test appearance.*